A Breakthrough Book
University of Missouri Press

Design for a House

Poems by Jonathan Holden

Acknowledgments

The Antioch Review: "El Paso"

The Beloit Poetry Journal: "The Genuine Article"

Bitterroot: "There Are Shadows so Full of Sadness"

The Massachusetts Review: "Hitting Against Mike Cutler";
  "Waking Up as a Child on a Summer Morning"

Northwest Review: "How to Have Fourth of July"

Poet Lore: "The Greenness"

"The Summer of Snakes" and "Breaking In" were first published
  in The North American Review, copyright © 1972 by the
  University of Northern Iowa.

ISBN 0–8262–0131–8 paper   ISBN 0–8262–0132–6 cloth

Library of Congress Catalog Number 72–84203

Printed in the United States of America

Copyright © 1972 by Jonathan Holden

For Richard Waidelich

The Devins Award for Poetry

Design for a House won, in manuscript,
The Devins Award for Poetry for 1972. A provision
of the Award—the major prize of the Kansas City Poetry
Contests—is publication by the University of Missouri Press.

Jonathan Holden's manuscript was chosen from several hundred
collections submitted anonymously by poets across the nation.
Judges for the 1972 competition were Carolyn Kizer, Donald
Finkel, and Bruce Cutler.

The annual Award is made possible by the generosity of
Dr. and Mrs. Edward A. Devins. Dr. Devins is former President
of the Kansas City Jewish Community Center and is a
patron of the Center's American Poets Series.

Contents

Design for a House, 11

Alone, 12

Apples, 13

April 1971, 14

Breaking In, 15

Dancing School, 17

Do I Dare to Eat a Peach, 18

Driving Down to Work, 19

Driving Through Coal Country in Pennsylvania, 21

El Paso, 22

Fire Building, 23

First Kiss, 24

Fishing as a Kid in the Black River, 25

The Genuine Article, 27

Goat Slaughter, 28

The Greenness, 29

Guns, 30

Hitting Against Mike Cutler, 32

How to Eat a Hot Fudge Sundae, 33

How to Have Fourth of July, 34

How to Make the Best Use of Fire, 35

How to Play Night Baseball, 36

How to Understand the Earth, 37

Ice Hockey, 40

In the Well of the Wordhoard, 42

Integrals, 43

It's Sunday Afternoon, 44

Moonwish, 45

Near Mendocino, 46

Night Campsite, 47

Night: Landing at Newark, 48

Pouring Concrete, 49

Cross Bracing, 50

Remembering My Father, 51

The Summer of Snakes, 52

There are Shadows so Full of Sadness, 54

Three Definitions of *Gaunt*, 55

Throwing My Boomerang, 56

Waking Up as a Child in a Thunderstorm, 57

Waking Up as a Child on a Summer Morning, 58

A War Baby Looks Back, 59

Wet Aspen, 60

After Building, 61

Design for a House

Design for a House

I've placed the windows so that
the shadows that eat across
the floor and the shadow of every
lonely stone and tree in the world
all lengthen together.

With the glass I'll use,
if you concentrate you can take
the warmth out of the sunlight
in your hands like a powder and softly
brush it wherever you want, across
the face of someone you love
or blow it into their eyes.

I'm inventing a new kind of
roof. Instead of flowing over
it, the shadows of clouds come
to roost. But you can scare them
away if it gets too dark—just by
snapping your fingers—flush the whole
flock of them, make them startle and
soar away on each other's heels.

And I've a new material for walls.
After it snows, go out
into their shadow: you can wade in the sky.

Alone

Alone is delicious.
There's no one to see.
I can eat these low clouds
and the body of wind
that's turning them into rolling
tumbleweed, eat with my hands,
get crumbs over everything,
crumbs of clouds on my nose,
in my fingernails, clouds smeared
all over my shirt and my chin,
I can lick the clouds off my fingers
and no one can see or care if
I have as much dessert as I want.
I just reach into those blue
holes that I've left and pull out
whole fistfuls of sky, of infinity.
It's tasteless and so hard
I can chew it for hours.

Apples

October. The orchard
in moonlight.
Surrounded by sticky bee-
chewed apples,
Georgia and I
lay on our thistly army
blanket, shivering.
As hard as I could
I hugged
her tinkertoy bones.
We lay like the two
halves of an apple
that's plummeted,
split, the moon
scouring us white,
the moist parts turning
brown.

April 1971

Now I know how dogs feel,
how after a summer shower the steam
from pavement smells. It's like
a woman's hair. Its fragrance
sticks, it drives you mad
as the smell of fresh bread
baking in the oven.

I can't eat yet.
But for the past three weeks
I've felt it coming. On windless
days I watch the dead grass listening.
Nothing can hold it back or dull
my hunger. I can't eat yet.
My teeth are all inside me, pushing.
I'm making bread.

The bread's in ferment, it
seethes. I have to wrestle it; it
clings to me, it sticks, rises
as it breathes. It's almost done.
The sun is coming out. The grass is
moving like a glossy pelt. The whole world
is warm, basking in the smell of baking bread.

Breaking In

1.
Tall, older than I,
that big kid on the mound
couldn't throw it through a
barn door. The whole barn
would cry, lie
softly down on itself in leaves.
He throws, but I can't see.
I'm just thankful I'm out,
on the bench again,
and only that barn is in pain.

2.
July. The Big Dipper is high.
I'm cold without my clothes.
I want to cover myself
with the blanket, but I can't.
She's older than I.
I hold one of her breasts
in my hand. It's dry
like a hornets' nest.
Why does she cry?

3.
The bat's too big for Eric.
I have to move up,
throw underhand. He
wallows at it, falls. The grass
nestles up to his ears. "Nice
try!" I call. And he picks himself
up. He believes me.

4.
She unhooks her bra. It
falls. Now she's all
there, as exposed to the air
as a raw, freshly skinned potato,
tremblingly earnest, out of
breath—not because she's
hot but because she's
never done this before. She
loves me. She's scared.
I'll have to hold her, try
and warm her slowly
slowly   slowly.

Dancing School

Marcia Thompane was light and compact,
her silk sides slick as fish's scales.
Doing the box step with me, she
stared into space, waiting
for somebody else.

Vernell Peterson was tense, rickety.
I had to crane up to speak
to her face. My fingers clung
to the rungs of her spine. Trying
to lead Vernell in the swing step
was like leading a dogwood tree.

Poor Liddy Morrison was always
the last to get picked. She was dense,
moist. An inner tube was tied
to her waist. Her gauze dresses
rasped like dry grass.
As I neared her, she'd stare
up with a dog's expectant look. I'd try
to be nice, to smile as though
I were glad it was her
I was stuck with; but Liddy
outdid me: she'd pretend
to be grateful.

Do I Dare to Eat a Peach

There's only one way to do it
that's fair to the peaches: sink
in your teeth, ravish them, the ripe ones
love it, they drool, they hurry to help
you undo them, to give up their pits, they
fall out all by themselves. If peaches
had voices, they'd cry, "Ah!" They kiss back
wildly, feed themselves further into
your mouth until it is full.

Driving Down to Work

Maybe a mile of dust
and spitting pebbles past
Stilsons' field with its little
horses that never look up
the car steps off the east
edge of the mountain into shade.
The plains are always out there
like the sea.

There's still snow here,
dead laundry on the side of the road.
I circle as I descend toward the first
switchback, hesitate at the top
of these stairs that plunge
as they curl out of sight.
I let my tires hesitate as they feel
their way around the inside track,
slither along licks of ice to scramble
back onto bare dirt. The car
succumbs. The plains
sink below the trees.

I enter new snow, new shadow,
where the light slips by in darts,
breast out into full brightness again
above the second switchback.
It's mercifully bare today, a sweaty
muck in which my tires make guzzling
chocolate sounds as they bank
left and steady out, sight
down the dodging rapids. I slosh
as I take each corner
in mincing little steps in second gear
before I let the reins out into third,
letting the brunt of the road rise up
and jog us a little as the tail of the curve
melts away, as the shadows flicker
and flee and we level out. The plains
are sinking again below the trees.

And I enter the easy stretch I know the best;
its abyss is coming in from the right,
the wall of rock on the left growing which started
toward me last month through falling snow
for no reason at all and then recoiled. My neighbor
spun the wheel. But the wall rushed us again,
missed. Someone is helping me do these slow
somersaults under water. At last we come up
for air. I'm on my back blinking up at the seat
I was just in, as the final tinkle of grinding
glass fades into this sudden
silence which I pass.

Driving Through Coal Country
    in Pennsylvania,

sometimes you come on a whole
valley that's one gray excavation.
Each valley saddens me.
It's like seeing someone you know
but can hardly recognize anymore,
scarred up, shaved, sick
from a long operation,
only the operation's still going on,
and there are no doctors—
just dump trucks in the distance
raising dust.

El Paso

The ragged graph of spiring crags
is chopped,
and there you are
littered in the valley below a quarry,
your offices rubbing elbows,
Juarez, like refuse, beyond.

It's too bright.
The land is gripping you
in the gritty palm of its hand,
the sun on its fingers.

The road from the north was a guitar string,
a streak in a dust-parched
ocean of swimming mountains.
It brought us to nothing.
And the river said to flow here is no consolation.

The only river is up
in a sky the color of gin.
The only ocean is dust,
the wash of its waves a lisp
of breeze through the heads of the cottonwood trees
and the tremor of jets from Biggs.

Except for the night,
when your halcyon baubles come on,
when your valley arrays itself like the coals of a hearth
and your hotel lights are as lonely as blue stratosphere,
you have one horizon:

it is the slice, the saw-toothed snarl
and scorch of the F-104's.

Fire Building

It's not easy
to make a fire

leap up in gusts.
It takes at least

two logs closely
crevassed over deep

coals. For each
fire lives to feel,

to be whole through
flames. But these

flames are eager
to live, these

flames leap and
are lonely.

First Kiss

The first girl I ever kissed was Sally Adams
on our third date. I was 13. I'd taken her
to *Battle Cry* with Aldo Ray.
Scarcely had the Looney Tunes cartoon come on
than we were in the usual position—
clutching hands, elbows, forearms all at once.
My left arm around her seat had gone to sleep,
when, silhouetted in the row in front,
this couple started wrestling in slow-motion.
You know how vampires, when they batten, fasten down?
That's what it looked like—on and on, his drooped head
lolling, rolling over hers until I thought, Ich!
Kissing that long's worse than holding hands; it's
messier! But I knew Sally saw them too. I
had to try. My heart began sprinting so hard
I was scared she heard it in my hot, tense hands.
To get across the space between two faces for the first
time's like standing on the high-dive, staring down.
You wish you'd jumped. You wonder if you'll dare.
My mouth was so dry I had to wet my lips. I sucked in
my breath, held it deep, launched out and down—
too late now to turn around—toward Sally's face, this
shy, dim crescent moon turning up toward me, becoming
full, with solemn eyes all filled with small, deep lights.
I heard distant gunshots, but I didn't care. I was
sinking. Her lashes grazed my cheek, and I realized
I was there. I'd landed not in a crash of water but
quietly, trembling, on the ground of this soft,
strange planet that seemed to move, to open under me.

Fishing as a Kid in the Black River

1.

There's a locust in my bike's
sprocket. It chirrs
as I coast. The wind is
paper rumpling in my ears,
the hot tar tears at my tires.
Then the air changes.
Jimmy and I are in the swamp,
our twin locusts shrill, as
shadow and sunlight swipe
at us, shadow and sun.

2.

I wouldn't drink the Black River.
Its bubbles don't move.
It's too quiet.
Even the sunlight that leaks
into it seems to get sick
as it fails, deep
in a dirty dusk of rotten
roots and ooze, vague bodies
where bloodsuckers live.

3.
The first night crawler's
a granddaddy. He keeps slipping
out of my fingers like somebody's
cool, greased lips. Puncturing him,
I prick my thumb with a white
bead of his guts, then double
the bleeding lips back as they're still
moving, trying to form an expression.

4.
Water splatters. Jimmy's
circuit's connected, his line is
thrilling with current, a sunfish
the size of a silvery sparrow
flittering its wings, splattering
water. Slimy as a wet
sliver of soap, it squirts
out of his hand
into the grass, arches,
floundering, gills
pulsing. We wait
as it pants. As it pants, as
it pants, its mouth
gaping in a stupid expression,
I can't help it: I think
of drowning.

The Genuine Article

Oh yes, the Acropolis is
the genuine article,
made from real stones
by genuine Greeks
in a century that is
traditional.

But if you wish
to remain closer to home,
for less cost, an old
Winchester 30-30
will do. A piece
of History, it won
the West by killing
guaranteed, naturally
toasted Indians. You don't
have to go far
from home.

For even less cost, try
a hot dog. It's
the genuine article.
Official American meat
clapped between airy
buns. It's almost real.

In fact, sometimes I think
that we
are the genuine article
though all we pay
to be
is the loneliness
we carry around,
and it comes wholesale
like the wind
absolutely free.

Goat Slaughter

W'aa! bawled the kid as they hauled it
tottering on twiggy legs toward the stock.
W'aa! He felt like I did when my mother
drove me to Dr. Lucas to have my teeth out
with gas. W'aa! The kid balked. With
gas. The rope jerked it forward. With
gas. Its mother crowded against the fence.
The nurse smiled at me, attached the bib.
Stuck in the stock, the kid waa'd louder.
Dr. Lucas's office smelled like sweet rubber.
The kid tried to yank its head back through
the hole, its ears got caught. W'aa! Everything
grew vague. They'd forced this sweet, roaring
rubber cup over my face: "Now breathe
deeply . . ." W'aa! Its hooves flailed and crashed
as they put the .22 between its eyes. "Now
breathe deeply . . ." W'aa! "Good . . .
Excellent . . ." I tried to get away. W'aa!
"Good . . . Excellent . . ." Pow, it collapsed,
kicking, and I woke up in a strange room,
spitting blood into a pan.

The Greenness

Once their eyes were beautiful,
and when the wind exhaled
it was warm as the insides of mouths
not yet kissed but dreamed.
The trees and grass flared up,
a flagrant green. What were you then
but a dog, sniffing,
beside itself with something on the wind?
No time at all before you found
others who'd take their clothes off in a room.
Their eyes were beautiful, and their breath was warm.
Their bodies bent like boughs in a summer storm,
but that was all. When they walked out the door,
the room was even emptier than before,
the green more bitter. You were grimmer, older.
You saw that what you'd dreamed was not the grass
but the greenness. Your own youth, slinking past
in a chrome Impala, gave you the cold shoulder.

Guns

Caps were illegal in New Jersey. I bought
all mine from friends who brought them back
from Florida. The guns we used were light
and tinselly. I wasn't supposed to point them
at my mother. Shot by one, you learned to
double up while staggering back, grimacing
and groaning. Winged, you clutched your arm.
"Creased" in the head enough to knock you out,
you closed your eyes and toppled slowly into
the dandelions.

Mr. Connon gave a wizened grin, testing the tin
can in his hand while I balanced myself unsteadily
under his 12-gauge shotgun, a catapult of shy, oiled
steel, the streamline thrust of its heft taking off
from my shoulder up into sheer power. "Ready?" He
threw. I pulled the trigger, flattened out the air
for a square mile with one blow that sent me staggering
back as the can, unharmed, landed on the lawn.

Grant Howell's parents weren't home. We'd spent
all afternoon trying to make ether by mixing car-battery
acid and rubbing alcohol. It wouldn't put us to sleep,
so Grant brought out his father's .25. The sky was gray.
Grant saw a robin balancing on a branch above the back
steps. He decided to shoot it. The pistol flinched
with a whap, but nothing happened. The robin balanced,
waiting. Whap! Whap! The .25 made its harmless,
popping reports. Whap! The robin barely blinked. Grant
got his father's .22, edged up under the branch, took long,
steady aim. The rifle spat a bristle of thin, dry echoes.
A feather fell off the robin. Reluctantly, the rest of it
lost its balance and landed in the mud. We threw it
in the bushes.

At a dude ranch in the Poconos I chaperoned the shooting
range for the senior boys' class trip. The rented rifles
were too light, they felt like toys, took only shorts that
snapped like caps. For a few hours, the boys shot at targets,
opened bolts together. Then one kid took off his hat, spun it
out in the dirt for all to shoot at. Whap! The hat jumped
and settled. Whap-whap-whap! It pulsed, still in one piece
punched all over with black dots. Whap-whap-whap! The hat
had lost its mind, was all tattered hole, air, bits of dirt
showing through, loose scraps of skin. It was not worth
shooting at anymore. "The frogs!" somebody shouted, "let's
get the frogs." The boys scattered with their guns into the
trees. For the rest of the afternoon, laughter and an occasional
thunk resounded from the swamp. Shortly after three
a stray bullet conked the barn 200 yards away. At five,
flushed with killing, we climbed aboard the bus for home.
Everybody was alive.

Hitting Against Mike Cutler

One down. I step into the narrow,
dust-floured shooting gallery, glance
out where the tall right-hander's squint
aims in to size things up. If it were up
to him, he'd take all afternoon he looks so
lazy—a gunslinger who just sauntered
into town, his jaw working over
a forgotten scrap of gum. He spits,
feels up the ball like a small, hard hornet;
and I hear the catcher settle in creaking
leather harness. He clucks contentedly,
does something dirty in his groin. Far
out there on the bright, bare, heat-rippling
hill the big guy nods. The hornet in his hand
begins to buzz. He bows. Slowly he
revolves away, then whirls, draws. I fire back.
The hornet hisses, vanishes with a BANG. STEE-RIKE!
The catcher grins. Good chuck, good chuck, he clucks.

How to Eat a Hot Fudge Sundae

Start with the
clouds. Eat
the clouds. Eat through
to the ground. Eat
the ground until you tap
the first, rich vein. Delve
from strata to strata
down into the cold, magma
core. Stir
the magma, pick up
the whole goblet, drink
straight from the goblet
until you've finished the world.

How to Have Fourth of July

    Use a sledge to smash each burlapped
bale of ice into wet jewels. With
whisky-soaked mint-leaves picked
that morning, pack this ice
into tall glasses until
you can scrape the frost off
with your nail. Pour on
the bourbon, drink
till your ears ring, your teeth
ache. Drink till your lips
are numb and you smell
the summer rain in a field filled
with fresh, wild mint.
    Never dunk cherry-bombs.
Under water they'll only go
boink! Light them on land
where their flash breaks the air
in half, bursts it like
a big bag leaving shorn edges
singed and smoking.
    When you slaughter the watermelons,
break off such hunks that when
you bite in you get water
all up your nose.
    And when it gets dark, don't go
to the fireworks. Go out into
sweet, cool thickets of
darkness, chase
the fireflies.
Clap them in jars until each jar
is inlaid with sleepy stars.

How to Make the Best Use of Fire

When you're hungry for heat
the coals of a fire are
fruit. I've picked apples,
tomatoes, ripe peaches, delectable
crimson cherries from coals, eaten
and spit out the ashes.
But the richest fires are
small, quick animals.
You draw out from under
the logs their organs—pink
kidneys, pink hearts still
leaping—you eat them alive.

How to Play Night Baseball

A pasture is best, freshly
mown so that by the time a grounder's
plowed through all that chewed, spit-out
grass to reach you, the ball
will be bruised with green kisses. Start
in the evening. Come
with a bad sunburn and smelling of chlorine,
water still crackling in your ears.
Play until the ball is khaki—
a movable piece of the twilight—
the girls' bare arms in the bleachers are pale,
and heat lightning jumps in the west. Play
until you can only see pop-ups,
and routine grounders get lost in
the sweet grass for extra bases.

How to Understand the Earth

1.

The topsoil has few bones.
My mattock cut that stuff
like steak. I chewed it
up until I bared the moist,
rare parts, devoured in
shovelfuls the earth's filet.
When roots began running
through in gristle strands
I hacked at them until they
sprang and I could stand
knee-deep in the wet meat
of the earth, the prongs
of hacked-off roots catching
at my dungarees, a fine
mud cooling on my face,
my arms still vibrant,
blossoming as I rested,
resting in my breathing,
tasting all the earth I'd moved
changed into air.

2.
No meat left.
The mattock blade bit off
peels of cold, gray butter.
As I slugged, the earth
tightened up, all
scar tissue now, tough fat
that sheared, leaving my
tooth marks, each cut
to be carved back slice
by slice until I started chinking
ice, smashing splinters up
into my face. I spit them
out, swung the pick's tooth
back into the pit to clang
on sparks that bounced back
my ringing weight. I swung,
rang sparks again,
the mattock shivered in my hand.
It was the earth's thick
skull I'd struck.

3.
Since my mattock head jarred
loose there's been nothing here
to eat but dust. For five days
I've been scarring the earth's
bones with this crowbar.
The ground refuses
to give way except in nicks and
pinches of white powder. I
am like water: the harder
the rock the slower,
the sheerer I cleave down.
I hoist the bar and let it fall
until, too tired to hoist
again, I sprawl on my belly,
reach down in and scrounge
around inside there with a trowel.
The rock is my adversary now.
I know him intimately.
I've found that if you
stay and fight him, bit by
bit he'll crack, give way
in little handfuls. I plan
to stay, to hit him, keep trying
to stun him again and again
until I win or I become
as numb as he.

Ice Hockey

Silver Lake has changed into a milky,
marble floor. Wind from around the bend
drives white dust up-ice with long broom-
strokes toward the dam. The lake
talks, mutters to itself as I take
my naked fingers out into air,
grab the laces, wind them round
my ankles, winch them so tight that my feet
wilt, then work back into my gloves.
I'm done: my fingertips are stones.
I lean, then, launch out over my stick
against the wall of the wind, make the whole
map of ice begin to move, the lightning-
splits of cracks begin to move
toward me, the sleek curves of other
skaters—etched with ice-spray where
their blades bit—begin to bend like moving
rails as the network of the city thins
to a few arcs across dark wilderness
where bubbles—the unblinking eyes
of fish—come flowing by. A loose
puck wobbles over the ripples.

I interrupt it, weave it with my wand,
let the wind into my lap to make me
stall, then with a willow flick
skim it back to the distant game,
follow it and join. The lake
begins to turn, a white wheel always
revolving, my legs robots, automatic,
kicking against the wheel
to make it spin until it streams so
fast my feet can't keep up, the wheel
flies out from under me, I sit down
hard on this slick seat that sears
my behind as it hisses to a halt,
then rise, chase down the game again,
thrust in my stick, grapple in the clatter.
The puck squirts free—in front of me—
alone, this rare coin, all mine.
I coddle it, nick the wheel, heave
at the wheel until it's whirling
under me in streaks, the goal swinging
into range, slap, miss, watch the puck
whiz, three guys stabbing after it
as I lean away into the force of ice
and level out, let the wind hit me
in the back and hurl me home again
across the fleeing map.

In the Well of the Wordhoard

the water is made
out of all the numbers which
haven't been tolled.
They wait there like owls
without eyes, hoot owls
which cannot hoot.

The whole sea is in there,
but its gulls can't whimper
or wheel; for the water
is made out of all the known
stars that have not yet learned
how to sob, or even to twinkle;
nor have the lakes ever been
bruised black by wind.

The lips of the lovers do not
know how to tiptoe to be tender.
The tigers do not know how
to roar, let alone burn.

Integrals

Erect, arched in disdain,
the integrals drift from left
across white windless pages
to the right,
serene as swans.
                    Tall,
beautiful seen from afar
on the wavering water, each
curves with the balanced severity
of a fine tool weighed in the palm.

Gaining energy now, they
break into a canter—stallions
bobbing the great crests of their manes.
No one suspects their power
who has not seen them rampage.
                    Like bulldozers, they build
by adding
            dirt to dirt to stumps added
                to boulders to broken glass added
                to live trees by the roots added
to hillsides, to whole
housing developments
                    that roll, foaming before them,
the tumbling end of a broken wave
in one mangled sum: dandelions, old
beer-cans and broken
windows—gravestones all
rolled into one.

Yes, with the use of tables
integration is as easy as that:
the mere squeeze of a trigger, no
second thought. The swans
cannot feel the pain
it happens so fast.

It's Sunday Afternoon

I've just stopped
thinking—to stare out
my window at San Francisco in
the sunlight like piles and
piles of sharp, bright rocks where
nothing moves except empty
cars and the clouds streaming in,
the wind's steady hiss like blowing
sand. They say we're living on
a planet, that it moves
through space, but I can see
no evidence for this. These bright
piles of rock are stuck right
here. Nothing ever really moves except
the wind nudging this house, my
wife creaking back and forth across
the floor, hardened to me, turning,
a distant planet. Nothing's
changed places except this dry
stuff that's drifting in
from somewhere, piling up
silently inside me like sand.

Moonwish

Tonight when I'm made
out of moonlight my
hands will be milk,
I'll drink up
my own fingers.

As frost creeps into
my valleys, I'll assume
the cold.
I'll stretch out, then,
so far that my muscles

are as hills,
the moon my navel,
and I live on the white
loaves of the mountains,
on my own arms.

Near Mendocino

I've basked in this wind before.
It makes the glossiest
grasses flash like wind
across water. All day it drove
clouds just like these—slow
herds of sheep—up from some
pasture not far to the west,
the dark smoke of their shadows
dimming, fleeing across the
diamond outside the window while
Mr. Snook talked about fractions
and I thumped and thumped my
feet, pined for recess. I don't
understand, then, why it is that
today, when I waded all morning
in glittering streams of grasses,
I should be this weary; why
I'm not sure where I live anymore
or if these clouds are fake.

Night Campsite

I can't sleep here. When the wind rises
through this rickety attic of pine
I wonder just how long it will be
before my own skin like this canvas
tent is torn right off me.
There's a lull, now, the tent
luffs; but I can hear the wind out
there foraging around in small platoons,
thrashing down the hill. Each group
of trees breaks into a shout
as the battle arrives, and I hear the mob
cry of trees to the west as the fight
spreads, tumbling nearer. The shout
rises. My insides cling together
again as the tent trembles, begins
beating, bursting out, gibbering.
The attic shakes, roars, strewing
debris, splinters, pine needles, twigs
across the fighting tent; the whole
ramshackle attic is swallowed in
the roar until it flags, and my huddled
insides relent and settle back to wait,
still warm under my skin.

Night: Landing at Newark

We're sinking into beds of lights that
roll over, come wallowing up
again to steady out as we descend
to the next level of the department
store, brush off a cloud into cosmetics
through women's lingerie out over dark
suits turning slowly back into jewelry, reaching
down into diamond tiepins, cuff links, soft
cloverleaves, white fur of the chemical
industry clinging to dreaming earth, dropping
a floor to women's shoes, men's hats, glaring
utensils, crowds of headlights folding
up as we sweep down the final escalator
into the fleeing basement's cement
hallway, wincing rubber
tires: I am home.

Pouring Concrete

The truck whined. The washing machine
of its belly began to revolve. It was
redigesting, it churned as it slowly
turned everything over again that was
going to come down the silver
children's slide that teetered
as we guided it into the trench;
and the smell of its food fumed up,
the smell of a washing machine
thrashing suds, a parched
cleanliness that would starch
every germ around in a split second,
of something trying to dry.
Water made the sun trickle as it
drooled down the slide, but I knew
now what the truck contained:
there was a desert inside.
For the last time in my life
I looked down at the dirt
I was standing on.

Cross Bracing

Anything that had studs or
that should stand straight
wobbled. Nails peeked out.
My tables trembled when I wrote.
My counters swayed. Heavily used,
they'd wallow until they'd worked
themselves back into the pieces
that I'd cut. I couldn't understand
why houses stood, until I learned
to cross brace, to notch 2 × 4's,
snap in the brace so that the slack
studs tensed together at attention.
Now, secretly, I sometimes lean
harder than I should against the things
I've built that stand, seize them
with a suddenness to make them
shake. They won't budge. They just
give me back this secret glee
of my own full weight. I would put
cross bracing into trees, in moving
clouds and water, into my whole
life if I knew how.

Remembering My Father

As I seize the ladder by its shoulder
blades and shake it back and forth
to test its roots, its cling, test
with gummed toes each rung up
from the shadow of the north wall
into the bright desert of the roof
the sun's weight spreads over my back,
and I see my father frowning in the sun,
his freckled back zigzagged with peeling
tan, his shoulders red, lowering a rock
into the stone swimming pool he built
by hand with boulders slithered
down on sledges from the woods,
split, rinsed off and fit—a pool
I could dive into until my ears
were so waterclogged they croaked.
I reach the top, fit
the window frame in place—the corners
mate—aim the first nail away
from the glass, sink it to its chin,
finger the next nail and prick
the wood; but as I heft the framing
hammer back to stroke, I see my father
in the cellar, frowning as he fits
his saw blade to a line, eases it back
and forth to start the cut, his breath
hissing through his nose as it always does
when he's intent. I hear my own breath
hissing through my nose. Something
silent in me starts chuckling in pure
gaiety because I'm frowning too, because
I know exactly what I look like.

The Summer of Snakes

The summer I turned ten was the summer of snakes.
Fearless, I stalked the Walters' field
where black snakes sunbathed on the hot, stone
foundation of the burned-down barn.
All summer in the grass I found them dead.
I wrapped their dry, flaked lengths around my neck,
whipped them through the air like black-snake whips.
Once I coiled a dead one, propped its head upon a forked
stick for Mrs. Emory to see when she came to give us
corn. She didn't scream. She turned white and made
gagging noises. Later, my mother lectured me.
"Mrs. Emory," she said, "is scared of snakes."
　　All summer long the snakes stretched out to dry.
One snake made his last mistake by
stretching out on the road in front of
Cissels' house. Mrs. Cissel had a baby. She lived
alone because Mr. Cissel had re-enlisted to fight
in the Korean War. He'd left her with a loaded .38.
Her hair was honey streaked with heavy cream.
Seeing the snake, I made my bike's brakes squeak,
then heard a clink—the milkman on Mrs. Cissel's
steps clinking the bottles as he climbed into his truck.
Worriedly, Mrs. Cissel smiled. They, too,
had seen the snake. Carefully, roaring his engine,
blossoming blue smoke, the milkman backed his truck,
aimed it at the sleeping snake, then lurched, bumped
over it hurriedly as if afraid it would bite, screech-braked.
Panting, the milkman chewed his gum importantly, his face
set like St. George. The snake was squished! In awed
approval, Mrs. Cissel gawked. Again the milkman backed,
lurched, again screech-braked, then revved. Grim,
without a backward glance or thanks he roared away.
I hated him.

I found fewer and fewer snakes after that. Two
weeks before school opened, the workmen came to fix
the road. I watched the smoking tar-truck creep along,
it sounded like a shower. Then the dump trucks blundered
by with sizzling gravel. And last the men, red-
faced and shiny, working rakes. I envied them
until they found the snakes—a whole nest
in the pipe by MacKenzies'. All that day, bolstered
by cold beer and with a savage, messianic zeal
they dragged floundering black snake after floundering
black snake from that pipe with the handles of their
rakes, slung the frightened snakes down and crushed
them with rocks until there were no more. Then,
tired but satisfied, they finished up the road.

Since that summer, there have been no more black snakes
in Walters' field.

There are Shadows so Full of Sadness

blue shadows on snow,
chaste shadows the
color of Sunday,

cold shadows the color of
loneliness filled

with the sound of
the wind when there's

no one to listen,

so full of the sound
of clouds   slowly

forever

coming to pieces over
the edge of high ridges

that when I look into
their blue eyes

to see who is
crying

they're empty.

Three Definitions of Gaunt

1.
Before snow,
when the black gestures
of the trees are paralyzed
against gray sky
and I can hear the honk
of distant diesel horns
I never heard before
from miles and miles
I know it's gaunt.

2.
As the two, wet worlds
of us loosen,
come apart, and I
come out of her and fall
limp, it's as though I pulled
my whole head out
into the thin sunshine
of late afternoon
still hungry for something,
still gaunt.

3.
When I reach
into running water
to clasp the trill
of the sun
I always miss,
my hand closes
on the water, comes
up with the gaunt.

Throwing My Boomerang

If a blade of this
boomerang hit a buck
deer in the head
he'd stagger and
sink to his knees.
I don't throw it at deer.
I throw at the air,
let it bank, skip off
as off water and
kick up its heels, go
galloping off,
swiping and nicking
the tips of the grass,
swoop up, whirl back . . .
All I care is
that I can catch my-
self again,
throw it back
at the air.

Waking Up as a Child in a Thunderstorm

Lightning!—just took
a black and white snapshot
of the cowboys on my wall
all bucking at once.
And there's a seam in
the sky that's creaking, coming
undone, caving in
far away. Lightning! I'm not
scared. I can hear the grass
outside drinking
and all the crickets
are out singing,
singing like mad.

Waking Up as a Child on a Summer Morning

Everybody should wake up like this:
their bed the deck of an ocean liner gliding
forward without a ripple past
these pale walls covered with
bucking cowboys toward the open
window where through the screen a breeze
comes softly in with roosters' calls.
It's still gray out, but I can tell
that somewhere under my bed, under
this house, this cellar, deep under-
ground there's a huge gear so
fine toothed, so smooth, so well
oiled and so
slow
you can hardly feel it turning
the sky like tons
of cold opal
over
into the sun.

A War Baby Looks Back

In the tender years of Eisenhower's first
term, I started mine
in Dr. Swain's office, my jaws pried wide,
my gums stuffed with cotton cigarettes,
staring sadly up into a soft, fluorescent
light while Dr. Swain peered down in
and frowned. I had to wear elastic bands
that caught in my mouth on steel hooks;
to wash my abhorrent, plastic bite-plate
off each night until my teeth were
straight. It was all worth it.
Thanks to Dr. Swain, one spring evening
toward the end of Eisenhower's second
term, on the cold leather of my parents'
car, a girl named Tina
let me feel her up.

Wet Aspen

The skins of these rainy aspen
have an adolescent glisten. This one

reminds me of a girl I've never seen,
her raw face smiling at me

on 14th St. in the rain, her eyes
sparkling, her cheeks bedraggled with

water, her hat dripping, her little
fingers jointed like aspen twigs about to

blossom, clinging to my arm, her lips
and her teeth steaming as she laughs.

I put my arms around the trunk, but it's too
thin, and the nubs on the bark are so

hard that they hurt. All the branches
tremble, shivering rain into my face, even

my feet are soaked. There's no sound except
the slow seep of rain through the misty woods.

After Building

I trust this chair because once
it was made out of boulders. This

room, when it rained,
formed gulleys. The walls

were made out of all
the separate battalions of wind

I could hear in the darkness
thrashing, slashing at every

tree as they marched
nearer. I can rely

on this floor now.
It used to drift.